Envenomators

DEADLY SPIDER BITE!

by Kevin Blake

Consultant: Professor Bryan Grieg Fry
Head of Venom Evolution Laboratory
School of Biological Sciences
University of Queensland, Australia

BEARPORT PUBLISHING

New York, New York

Credits
Cover, © John Cancalosi/Alamy; 3, © Holger Kirk/Shutterstock; 4L, © Densey Clyne/Nature Production/
Minden Pictures; 4R, © Caters News Agency; 5L, © Michael Doe; 5R, © James van den Broek/Shutterstock;
6, © mjmediabox/Alamy; 7, © Caters News Agency; 8, © DenisVesely/iStock; 9T, © Nathanael Siders/
Shutterstock; 9B, © Ksenia Lada/Shutterstock; 10, © Kent, Breck P./Animals Animals–Earth Scenes; 11T, © Phil
Degginger/Alamy; 11B, © Robert D Brozek/Alamy; 12L, © JE1/Judy Eddy/WENN/Newscom; 12R, © Miles
Boyer/Shutterstock; 13, © Meghan Linsey/Mount Music Group; 14, © Meghan Linsey/Mount Music
Group; 15, © Blend Images/Alamy; 16L, © Jackson Landers; 16R, © Mark Gottlieb/VWPics/Redux Pictures;
17, © Robinson, James/Animals Animals–Earth Scenes; 18L, © REDPIXEL.PL/Shutterstock; 18R, © Welcome
Collection/CC BY 4.0; 19, © Sean Prior/Alamy; 20L, © Tim Faulkner; 20R, © Mark Moffett/Minden Pictures;
21, © imageBROKER/Alamy; 22 (L to R), © James van den Broek/Shutterstock, © Sari Oneal/Shutterstock,
and © Jack Glisson/Alamy.

Publisher: Kenn Goin
Senior Editor: Joyce Tavolacci
Creative Director: Spencer Brinker
Photo Researcher: Thomas Persano

Library of Congress Cataloging-in-Publication Data

Names: Blake, Kevin, 1978– author.
Title: Deadly spider bite! / by Kevin Blake.
Description: New York, New York : Bearport Publishing, [2019] | Series:
 Envenomators | Includes bibliographical references
 and index.
Identifiers: LCCN 2018014141 (print) | LCCN 2018017002 (ebook) |
 ISBN 9781684027026 (ebook) | ISBN 9781684026562 (library)
Subjects: LCSH: Poisonous spiders—Juvenile literature. |
 Spiders—Venom—Juvenile literature.
Classification: LCC QL458.4 (ebook) | LCC QL458.4 .B636 2019 (print) |
 DDC 595.4/4165—dc23
LC record available at https://lccn.loc.gov/2018014141

For more information, write to Bearport Publishing Company, Inc., 45 West
21st Street, Suite 3B, New York, New York 10010. Printed in the United States
of America.

10 9 8 7 6 5 4 3 2 1

Contents

Night Attack

It was December 2017 in New South Wales, Australia. Fiona Donagh was asleep in her bed when she felt something crawling up her leg. What Fiona didn't yet know was that a **venomous** Sydney funnel-web spider was hiding under her sheets. Without looking, she shook her leg. Fiona felt a burst of burning pain. The frightened spider had plunged its fangs into her body.

A Sydney funnel-web spider

Fiona Donagh lives in Australia, which is home to several kinds of venomous spiders.

Fiona sprang out of bed, switched on the light, and immediately saw the spider. She grabbed a glass bowl and trapped the spider under it. Within seconds, the creature's venom had spread throughout Fiona's body. She felt like her **flesh** was on fire.

A close-up view of a funnel-web spider's fangs and drops of venom

Sydney funnel-web spiders are about 2 inches (5 cm) long and are known for their tube-shaped webs. They are among the most venomous spiders in the world.

Fighting to Survive

Fiona grabbed her phone and called for help. As she did so, her **symptoms** worsencd. "My lips started to go numb and tingly, and I could feel it spreading around my face and my tongue," Fiona said. Then she began to drool, and her muscles twitched uncontrollably. Minutes later, an ambulance arrived at her home. On the way to the hospital, Fiona wondered: *Am I going to die?*

Fiona passed out in the ambulance on her way to the hospital.

At the hospital, doctors examined the spider, which Fiona had put in a jar. It was, in fact, a Sydney funnel-web spider. The doctors acted quickly, giving Fiona two doses of **antivenom**. Eventually, she began to recover. Fiona was very thankful to be alive. Without antivenom, a bite from a funnel-web spider can kill a person within an hour!

Yorick, the Sydney funnel-web spider that bit Fiona

After capturing the spider in a jar, Fiona named the creature Yorick. It died when a nurse accidentally stabbed it while trying to poke air holes in the jar.

"I'm not a fan of spiders, but I am aware it was not an intentional attack," says Fiona.

Hungry Spiders

While all of Earth's approximately 45,700 different **species** of spiders have venom, very few are dangerous to people. In fact, most spiders' fangs are too short to **penetrate** human skin. Even when spiders do bite, their venom usually isn't strong enough to make people sick. The venom is most effective on the small animals, such as insects, that spiders hunt.

Spiders belong to a group of animals called arachnids (uh-RAK-nids). All arachnids have two main body parts and eight legs.

A spider **injects** venom into its **prey** through hollow fangs connected to special venom **glands**. Once injected, the venom quickly **paralyzes** the prey's body. The spider then begins to feed on its victim, often while the animal is still alive!

A spider produces juices that turn its food into mush. Then it slurps up its liquid meal.

Spiders also use their venom to fight off **predators**, such as lizards and frogs.

Pick Your Poison

Not all spider venom works the same way. For example, funnel-web and black widow spiders have neurotoxic (NU-roh-tox-ik) venom, which attacks a person's **nervous system**. This type of venom causes pain, sweating, muscle cramps, and vomiting—and can even affect heart function.

A black widow spider

Spiders sometimes give a "dry bite." That's what happens when a spider sinks its fangs into its victim but doesn't inject anything.

Other spiders, such as the brown recluse spider, make what's known as **necrotic** venom. This type of venom kills **tissue**. Over time, the flesh surrounding the bite area blackens and dies. Bite victims are often left with nasty scars.

The brown recluse's venom can cause pain and vomiting and destroy tissue.

A necrotic spider bite

Bitten!

American country musician Meghan Linsey discovered the dangers of necrotic spider venom for herself. One morning in February 2017, Meghan felt an "**intense** stinging feeling" on her cheek. When she awoke, she found a large, dying brown recluse spider in her hand, which she had swatted during the night.

Meghan Linsey

A brown recluse spider like the one that bit Meghan

The brown recluse spider lives in the midwestern United States. It's one of the most venomous spiders in the world.

Meghan put the dead spider in a bag and rushed off to the doctor. Even with medical help, Meghan had nine days of what she called "crazy, crazy symptoms." Flat red bumps appeared on her body. Pain shot through her face, all the way down to her shoulder blades. Her cheek swelled so much that she could barely see out of her left eye. The worst was yet to come, however.

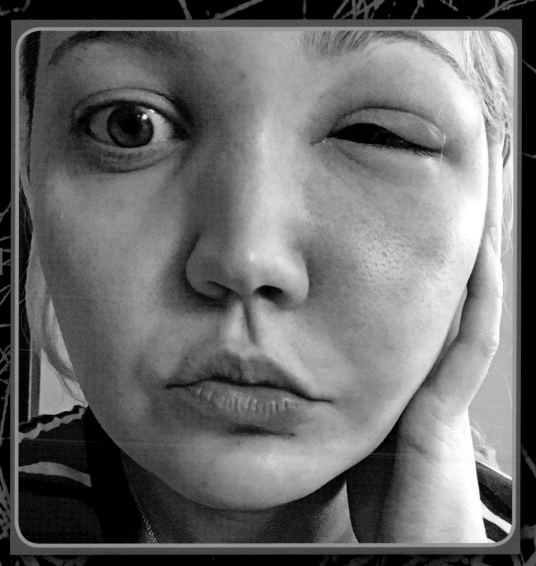

The spider's venom caused severe swelling in Meghan's face.

Rotting Flesh

The ninth day after her spider encounter, Meghan looked in the mirror and saw something terrifying. The skin where she had been bitten was turning a **gruesome** dark color. The powerful necrotic poison had killed a patch of tissue on her face! The dead, rotting black skin grew into a **lesion** so large that it looked, says Meghan, like "a hole on my face."

The dying skin around Meghan's eye

14

Doctors gave Meghan a special cream to help heal the wound. Over many days, the hole in Meghan's face began to shrink. After surviving the horrible bite, Meghan says, "I am so incredibly grateful for my health, and I will never take it for granted again."

Meghan was treated inside a special compartment filled with oxygen called a hyperbaric (hye-per-BAR-ik) chamber. This is often used to help heal serious wounds.

There is no antivenom for a brown recluse spider's venom.

A Wrong Step

Meghan was bitten by one of the two most venomous spiders in the United States. The other one—the black widow spider—sank its fangs into nature writer Jackson Landers. One warm afternoon in 2013, Jackson slipped his feet into a pair of shoes he had left on his porch. It wasn't long before he felt his toe sting. "At first, I thought maybe I had a thorn or something in the shoe," Jackson says. "And then, it got worse."

Black widow spiders get their name from the fact that females sometimes kill the males after mating.

Jackson Landers lives in Charlottesville, Virginia.

Black widows live in many places around the world. The female black widow spider is more deadly and has a red hourglass pattern on her body.

Sitting down on a rock, Jackson removed his shoe and found a squished black widow spider inside. Not knowing how severe the bite was, Jackson walked down to a nearby lake to fish. Soon, a warm feeling started to spread through his body, and his stomach began to hurt. At that moment, he knew he had to go to the hospital.

female

male

Female black widows are bigger and more venomous than the males. They also have longer fangs, which can inject venom deeper into their prey.

Antivenom

On his way to the hospital, Jackson said the pain "was like a **vise** grabbing my **abdomen** and squeezing." At the hospital, as doctors examined the bite, Jackson **clenched** his teeth to deal with the horrible pain he was feeling. Doctors injected him with a new kind of antivenom. "It was this incredible, magical warmth that spread through my arm . . . as pain was erased," he now remembers. Jackson, thankfully, made a full recovery.

Albert Calmette

Antivenom was discovered over 100 years ago by French doctor Albert Calmette.

So what is antivenom, and how is it made? Most often, it's made from horse blood! Scientists carefully inject a horse with tiny amounts of spider venom. Then they wait until the animal's body produces **antibodies** powerful enough to fight the venom. Scientists remove those antibodies from the horse's blood and give the **substance** to people who have been bitten by venomous spiders.

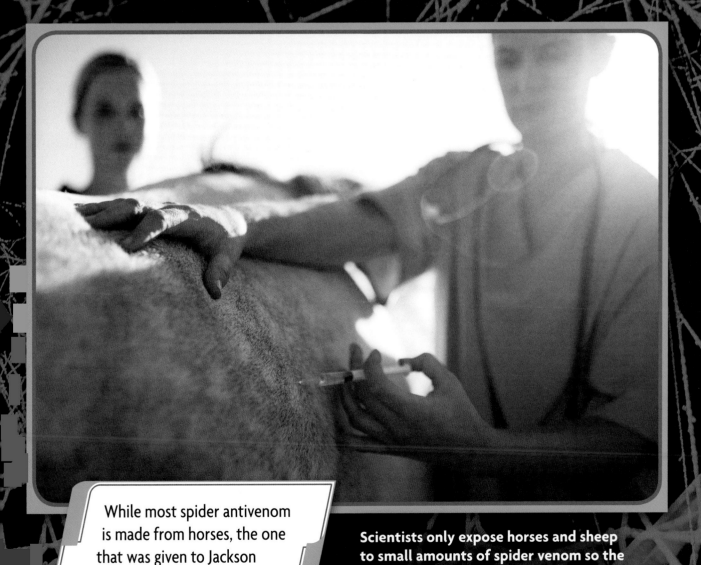

While most spider antivenom is made from horses, the one that was given to Jackson came from sheep.

Scientists only expose horses and sheep to small amounts of spider venom so the animals are not put in any real danger.

Searching for Spiders

Making antivenom isn't an easy process. In some places, hospitals don't have enough of the lifesaving medicine. In response, Tim Faulkner, the manager at an Australian wildlife park, asked people in his community to help capture deadly funnel-web spiders in order to make more antivenom. "We have tried to catch enough spiders ourselves and we just can't," Tim said. "We rely on community support."

Tim Faulkner

Scientists use special plastic test tubes to capture the spiders.

Scientists "milk" funnel-web spiders for their venom, which is used to create antivenom. Milking does not hurt the creatures.

However, Tim warns: "Please don't touch them. Don't try to pick them up." Instead, he recommends using a glass jar, which is something that the spider's fangs can't break through. "Catching venomous spiders is safe, as long as **precautions** are followed," Tim says. "We've been doing this for 35 years, and no one's been hurt."

Spiders should never be handled.

Venomous Spiders
—PROFILES—

	Black Widow Spider	Brown Recluse Spider	Sydney Funnel-Web Spider

DESCRIPTION	Black widow spiders range from reddish brown to black in color. The more dangerous female is usually a shiny black, with a red hourglass marking on her body.	In addition to being brown, these spiders can be white, gray, or black. Sometimes, they have a marking that looks like the outline of a violin on their backs.	Sydney funnel-web spiders have dark-colored bodies. Their long fangs enable them to inject venom deep into their prey.
LENGTH	0.12 to 1.5 inches (0.3 to 3.8 cm)	0.2 to 0.8 inches (0.5 to 2 cm)	About 2 inches (5 cm)
VENOM and Its Effects	The venom from a female black widow can cause severe muscle pains, rapid heartbeat, and twitching. The bite from the weaker male black widow, however, causes few symptoms.	While the brown recluse bite isn't as painful as that of other spiders, it can be even more dangerous. Its necrotic venom kills tissue, often leaving deep lesions and scars.	Along with extreme pain, the funnel-web spider's venom can cause sweating, twitching, drooling, and even death. The venom of the male spider is up to six times more powerful than that of the female.

Glossary

abdomen (AB-duh-muhn) the part of a person's body between the chest and hips

antibodies (AN-tee-bod-eez) substances in the blood that help fight disease and poisons

antivenom (an-tee-VEN-uhm) a medicine that blocks the effects of venom

clenched (KLENCHD) squeezed tightly

flesh (FLESH) the soft parts of a human body, including muscle and fat

glands (GLANDZ) body parts that produce chemicals

gruesome (GROO-suhm) horrible

injects (in-JEKS) forces, often a liquid, into another object

intense (in-TENSS) very strong

lesion (LEE-zhun) an area on the body that has suffered damage

necrotic (nuh-KRAH-tik) causing the death of cells in a body part

nervous system (NUR-vuhss SIS-tuhm) a system that carries instructions between the brain and the rest of the body

paralyzes (PA-ruh-lize-iz) causes something to be unable to move

penetrate (PEN-uh-trate) to go inside

precautions (pree-KAW-shunz) things done in advance to prevent something dangerous or unpleasant from happening

predators (PRED-uh-turz) animals that hunt and eat other animals

prey (PRAY) an animal that is hunted by another animal for food

species (SPEE-seez) groups that animals are divided into, according to similar characteristics

substance (SUHB-stuhnss) a particular kind of matter

symptoms (SIMP-tuhmz) signs of a disease or other physical problem felt by a person

tissue (TISH-oo) a group of specialized cells, such as skin

venomous (VEN-uhm-uhss) full of toxic substances

vise (VYSE) a metal tool that holds an object firmly in place

Index

Bibliography

Guarino, Ben. "Zoo to Australians: Please Help Us Catch Deadly Funnel-Web Spiders." *The Washington Post* (January 26, 2017).

Landers, Jackson. "Dancing with Black Widow Spiders." *The New York Times* (September 16, 2013).

Read More

Blake, Kevin. *Deadly Scorpion Sting! (Envenomators).* New York: Bearport (2019).

Lunis, Natalie. *Deadly Black Widows (No Backbone!).* New York: Bearport (2009).

Learn More Online

To learn more about venomous spiders, visit
www.bearportpublishing.com/Envenomators

About the Author

Kevin Blake lives in Providence, Rhode Island,
with his wife and children. He has written
many nonfiction books for kids.